PRESENTED BY

Henry Bowden
1996

In memory
of
Ellen █. Fleming
Bowden

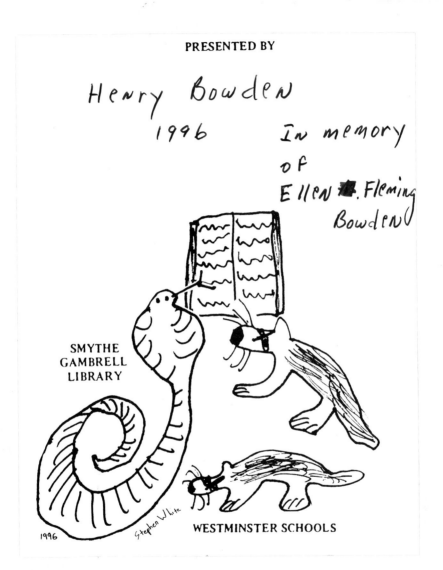

SMYTHE
GAMBRELL
LIBRARY

WESTMINSTER SCHOOLS

1996

Stephen White

MAIL CALL!

MAIL CALL!

THE HISTORY OF THE U.S. POSTAL SERVICE

BY
NANCY O'KEEFE BOLICK

A FIRST BOOK

FRANKLIN WATTS
NEW YORK   CHICAGO   LONDON   TORONTO   SYDNEY

Cover illustration by Steve Savage

Photographs copyright ©: UPI/Bettmann: pp.2, 13, 44; The Bettmann
Archive: pp. 8, 26, 33, 34, 47; North Wind Picture Archives, Alfred, Me.:
pp. 10, 17, 22, 27, 36, 38, 40, 42, 45; New York Public Library, Picture
Collection: p. 14; U. S. Department of Transportation, Federal Highway
Administration: pp. 19, 20, 29; Archive Photos: pp. 24 (both Kean), 31;
United States Postal Service: pp. 48, 49, 50, 53, 55; National Postal
Museum, The Smithsonian Institution: p. 59 #(86-4439).

Library of Congress Cataloging-in-Publication Data
Bolick, Nancy O'Keefe.
Mail Call! : the history of the U.S. Postal Service /
Nancy O'Keefe Bolick.
p. cm. — (A First book)
Includes bibliographical references and index.
ISBN 0-531-20170-8
1. Postal service — United States — History — Juvenile litera-
ture. [1. Postal service — History.] I. Title. II. Series.
HE6371.B65 1994
383'.4973 — dc20   94-49
CIP AC

CONTENTS

INTRODUCTION

Can you name one person who visits your house every day of the week—except Sundays and holidays?

This visitor delivers party invitations, birthday presents, letters from your relatives, packages, and bills for your parents. No matter who you are, or where you live, or how often you move, there's a person like this in your life.

Who is this friend who makes the rounds through rain and shine, snow and sleet, day after day? Your mail carrier, of course.

Mail carriers work for the United States Postal Service. You can see them in their familiar blue uniforms walking or driving mail Jeeps through your neighborhood. At the post office, you meet postal

Mail carriers laden with 1952 Christmas packages and cards head out of the main post office in New York City.

clerks who sell stamps, weigh packages, and sort the mail.

Every day, thousands of men and women pick up and deliver the letters and packages that keep our country running. People just like them have been doing the same job for more than two hundred years.

The Postal Service is as old as the United States. This is its story.

CHAPTER 1

EARLY DAYS IN THE COLONIES

Staying in touch with other people is easy these days. We can call friends on the telephone. Television and radio quickly tell us what is happening all around the world. Fast mail service gets our letters to their destinations often overnight. Magazines are delivered to homes soon after they are printed. We can even fax letters over telephone lines and write to other people using electronic mail, or e-mail, through computers. Communication has never been so fast, easy, and affordable.

It wasn't always this way. Try to imagine yourself as one of the first American colonists. It took you several months to sail from England to North America. When you got here, all you could see were trees, rivers, hills, and wide-open spaces. There was no way to communicate with anyone but the people right around

This engraving from a painting by the acclaimed
nineteenth-century artist Howard Pyle shows
a busy seaport in colonial America.

you. But you wanted to stay in touch with family and old friends back home and with new friends who moved on to different settlements in the Americas. Like people everywhere, you had things to say and people to say them to. You needed a mail system.

The urge to reach out to other people is as old as history. The earliest letter we know about was written on clay tablets in Babylonia more than four thousand years ago. People have written letters on parchment, on tribal message sticks, even on feathers.

In the fifth century B.C., Herodotus, a Greek philosopher, wrote of men on horseback who carried bronze tablets with messages written on them. Seeing these messengers inspired him to write the line that was later inscribed over the main entrance of the New York City General Post Office: "Neither snow, nor rain, nor heat, nor gloom of night stays these couriers from the swift completion of their appointed rounds."

Cultures before ours worked out many ways of moving the mail. In Rome during the third century B.C., it was carried on horseback. In the eighth century A.D., Arabs used carrier pigeons.

Speed was always important. In the fifteenth century, the French king Louis II was so eager to get the mail through that a delay could mean extreme punishment, even death, for the carrier.

Early European postal services, such as those in

sixteenth-century Austria, Germany, and England, were so expensive to use that only royalty and the very rich could afford the cost of mailing.

Mail service began in the American colonies in 1639, when the General Court of Massachusetts designated a Boston tavern as the first official drop for mail coming or going overseas. Other colonies along the East Coast worked out their own systems. In the South, slaves delivered messages from one plantation to another. In all of these arrangements, the mail got through—sort of.

The system became more centralized in 1691 when England took charge of delivering mail in all the colonies. The British government appointed the official postmaster and oversaw the operation from England.

It wasn't until the American Revolution that the mail system as we know it now really began. On July 26, 1775, the Second Continental Congress agreed that there should be a postmaster general of the United States.

The new country was on its own, and the postmaster general, headquartered in Philadelphia, Pennsylvania, would have the authority to run a national mail system. Benjamin Franklin, the first man appointed to the job, would come to be known as the Father of the U.S. Postal Service.

Above the entrance to the main post office in New York are the famous words "Neither snow, nor rain, nor heat, nor gloom of night stays these couriers from the swift completion of their appointed rounds."

The first post office in America for the
collection of mail was established on
November 5, 1639, in Boston.

CHAPTER 2

BENJAMIN FRANKLIN: FATHER OF THE U.S. POSTAL SERVICE

You probably know a few things about Benjamin Franklin. His famous kite experiments with lightning led him to think that wonderful things could be done with electricity. He designed bifocal glasses to help people see better. He invented the Franklin stove to heat homes.

He mapped the mysterious Gulf Stream for faster mail routes to England and organized America's first hospital and volunteer fire brigade. He also helped to write the Declaration of Independence, and persuaded France to help the colonies break away from England. No wonder he was just about the most popular man in America in the 1700s.

Ben Franklin also knew quite a bit about mail and how to deliver it in the colonies. He was officially named postmaster general of the United States when the job—and the new country—were created in 1775. But his involvement with the postal service started long before that, in the colonial days when the system was run by the British.

Franklin was born in 1706, when there were only about 250,000 people in all the colonies. Most of them lived in Boston, Connecticut and New York, Maryland and Virginia, and Charleston, Carolina. Settlements were connected by roads that weren't much better than paths. Ferries, not bridges, took people over rivers. Mail delivery was slow and uncertain.

Franklin was named postmaster of Philadelphia in 1737. He was thirty-one years old then, a printer and publisher of a newspaper called *The Pennsylvania Gazette*. The postal job was part-time, and Franklin was just one of many men employed by England to move the mail in the colonies.

In 1753, Franklin became co–postmaster general for the Crown for all the colonies. Right away, he began traveling to inspect northern post offices and those in Maryland and Virginia to learn how the system worked. In those days, mail in the colonies was carried over rutted paths and on rivers and streams, and Franklin could see that delivering it was a difficult job.

The inventive Franklin came up with many new ideas for speeding up mail delivery. He ordered new

Benjamin Franklin, the father of the United States Postal Service

land surveys and mapped out the post roads—shorter direct routes that cut travel time.

On his tour of post offices, Franklin learned that every postmaster had his own way of bookkeeping. He wrote new regulations and designed forms that made accounting the same everywhere. He increased delivery from one to three times a week in the summer (twice a week in cold months) between New York and Philadelphia, and to twice a week between Philadelphia and Boston. With these improvements, the postal system started making money.

To sort letters faster, Franklin designed cases with small holes, one for each destination. He set out milestones—stone markers—to show distances on the post roads so carriers could judge how far they traveled. That was important, because they earned three pennies a mile (1.6 km) in summer and three and a half pennies in winter to gallop over the countryside on their horses.

As the colonists moved toward a break with England, the Continental Congress, like Franklin, believed that a good mail system would make it easier for the scattered colonies to unite their common goal of achieving independence. In fact, during the Revolutionary War, politicians from different parts of the country and military men serving away from home would depend on the mail more than anyone else. Postmasters and post riders would be considered so valuable for the messages they delivered that they didn't have to serve in the military.

As events led up to the Revolution, the colonists lost trust in a postal system controlled by the British. The British, too, were wary. Suspecting Franklin of

Benjamin Franklin traveled through the colonies to gather information for his report to the Continental Congress on establishing a postal system.

being too sympathetic to the colonists, the Crown fired him in 1774, and the system he had developed began to fall apart.

The next spring, in May 1775, delegates from all the colonies met at the Continental Congress in Philadelphia to decide how to shape a new government. Among the main issues before them was how to keep the mail moving.

Naturally, the convention turned to the experienced Franklin for an answer. They named him chairman of a Committee of Investigation and asked him to set up a workable postal system that would be run by the national government. On July 26, only two months later, Franklin reported back to the convention with a plan. A day later, he was appointed the first postmaster general under the Continental Congress, a post he held until November 1776.

By the time Ben Franklin left office, post roads ran from Maine to Florida, from New York

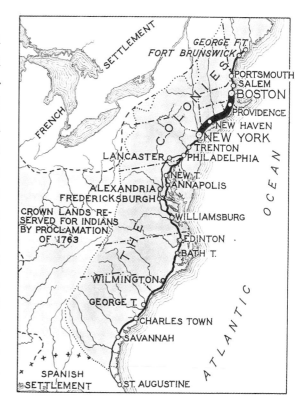

Post roads spanned the length of the Atlantic Coast, from Maine to Florida.

to Canada, and a dependable schedule operated between the colonies and England. Customers enjoyed regular deliveries along scheduled routes. They could count on the mail during a time when there was no other way to communicate over long distances.

CHAPTER 3

THE NEW NATION

In 1778, the Articles of Confederation granted the Continental Congress the official right to run the postal system. Article IX gave the Congress "the sole and exclusive right and power" to establish and regulate "post offices from one State to another" and to exact "such postage on papers passing through the same as may be requisite to defray the expenses of the said office. . . ."

The new system was based in Philadelphia. It started small, with a postmaster general, a secretary/comptroller, three surveyors, one inspector of dead letters, and twenty-six post riders. There were seventy-five post offices and about 2,400 miles (3,900 km) of post roads serving three million people.

On September 26, 1789, President George Wash-

Post riders carried mail along the new
post roads between colonial cities.

ington named Samuel Osgood of Massachusetts the first postmaster general under the new federal Constitution. It didn't take Osgood long to discover that some things had to change if the postal service was to make money for the new government.

The first problem was that anyone could carry letters and dispatches and there was no schedule. The second was that ship captains carrying mail from overseas did not have to deliver the mail to a post office. In both cases, there was no revenue for the government.

Congress finally set postal rates in 1792. These rates were based on how far a letter traveled. The charge was six cents for a one-page letter going as far as 30 miles (48 km) and up to twenty-five cents for one going 450 miles (725 km). Congress gave itself the authority to map out post roads and ruled that the system had to support itself and use its profits to expand service.

Within a short time, in 1794, the first letter carriers appeared on the streets of some cities, dropping mail at individual houses and businesses just as postal workers do today. They did not earn a salary from the postal department, however. Instead, they collected two cents from the recipient for each piece of mail they delivered. That did not change until more than sixty years later, when mail delivery became free

Samuel Osgood (left) and Gideon Granger (right)

to those who received it, because postage was paid by the sender.

In 1808, New York became the first city to establish a post office. Postmaster Gideon Granger advocated the idea of a central place where letters could be safely kept. He cautioned, however, that it was unlikely that there would be so much business that a whole room would have to be set aside for mail storage. Just as good in most cases, he said, was a plain case or a pine desk with a good lock and key.

CHAPTER 4

MOVING
THE MAIL

Load letters on mule teams. Move them by stagecoach. Pack them in railroad cars and steamboats. How about balloons, dog sleds, rockets, homing pigeons—or camels? The postal service tried them all, servicing settlers as they moved westward.

Delivering mail was always hard work. During the American Revolution, riders on horseback carried messages from the constantly moving military headquarters to soldiers in the battlefield, as well as from the soldiers to their families back home. The mail carriers dodged bullets and faced bad weather to get the mail through.

After the Revolution, cities such as Boston, New York, and Philadelphia grew into centers of com-

Dogsleds were among the more innovative means used by the post office to deliver mail under difficult conditions.

merce, trade, shipping, and entertainment. People needed to send legal papers, notices, letters, and newspapers to business associates, friends, and family members.

In 1799, the government jumped into the overland coach business to move mail between Philadelphia and New York. Because the horse-drawn coaches stopped at designated points along the route to pick up and discharge passengers and mail, moving in stages along the way, they became known as stage-coaches.

POST CHAISE LINE,

FOR PHILADELPHIA,
VIA STATEN-ISLAND.
Through in one day, and by daylight, with superior accommodations.

The most sure and safe conveyance between the two cities.

A CHAISE will leave the office No. 145 Broadway, a few doors above the City Hotel, every morning at 5 o'clock in the Vice-President's Steamboat NAUTILUS, by way of Staten-Island, Woodbridge, New-Brunswick, Princeton, Trenton, and Bristol, and arrive in Philadelphia at 5 o'clock the same evening.

The Proprietors of the above line have been particular in selecting good and careful drivers, new carriages, and superior horses, and therefore trust the public will be much gratified after travelling this route.

For seats in the above line, apply at the office No. 145 Broadway, No. 5 Courtlandt-street, at the Steamboat Hotel, corner of Marketfield and Washington-streets, J. & C. Seguine's, Whitehall, or to Capt. De Forest, on board the Steamboat Nautilus, at Whitehall-slip.

. All goods and baggage at the risk of the owners.

A Chaise will convey the Passengers to and from their respective Lodgings in each City, free of expense.

JAMES GUYON, jun. } Proprietors,
CALEB T. WARD, } New-York.
ROBERT LETSON, New-Brunswick.
JOHN JOLINE, } Princeton.
JOS. B. GROVER, }
JOSEPH I. THOMPSON, } Philadelphia.
DAVID BRENTON, }
July, 1810. E. W. MILLS, Agent for Proprietors.

This handbill was used to advertise
stagecoach services in the
early nineteenth century.

There was money to be made moving passengers, but not in carrying the mail. The stagecoach era floundered on poor service, irregular schedules, and broken contracts. In the early 1800s a new invention, the steamboat, began moving mail along rivers and the canals that were being built to connect the rivers. In 1813, Congress declared all steamship lines post routes and extended federal jurisdiction over them.

In time, as railroads began connecting eastern cities, trains replaced steamboats as the fastest means of moving the mail. In 1838, Congress declared that railways were post routes, too. For the better part of the nineteenth century, trains carried most of the country's mail.

Railroads were important to the growth of the country, particularly in the West. The Post Office relied on them as well. Soon towns grew up around whistle-stops where mail was deposited for distribution to the surrounding countryside. But the railroads had a monopoly, and they knew it. They were constantly raising prices and bickering with the postal service.

That ended, however, in 1845, when the federal government created the "star route" contractor system and hired private companies to carry the mail between major points. Now many companies bid for the business of moving mail over highways and waterways.

Through the history of the postal service there

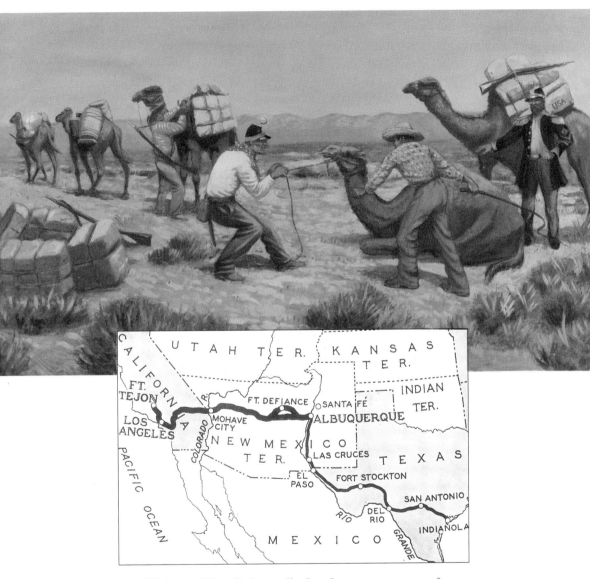

These "Ships of the Sahara," also known as camels, were used in the American Southwest to deliver the mail. The map inset shows the route followed by the camels.

have also been some unusual transportation alternatives. In 1855, Jefferson Davis got Congress to appropriate $30,000 to buy camels for the Army. It was a romantic notion to equip soldiers, post office employees, and private carriers to ride those "Ships of the Sahara" over southwestern deserts. The camels and riders followed an old mail road from Fort Pejon in Tehachapis to Los Angeles. Although the camels adapted well, people lost interest in them within a couple of years, and their use was discontinued.

Balloon delivery? John Jeffries soared from England to France in a balloon in 1785, carrying a letter from Ben Franklin.

Later, the Post Office became intrigued with the notion of heavier-than-air flight. In 1911, a special carrier, Earle Ovington, flew the first experimental air routes in New York State, from Garden City to Mineola. Ovington circled the Mineola airfield as he unloaded mail sacks to the postmaster, waiting below.

The Post Office authorized more flights all over the country, and eventually Congress authorized $100,000 to establish permanent routes in 1918. Regular air postal service began on May 15, 1918, when a letter from President Woodrow Wilson was flown from Washington, D.C., to New York. Because there were no radios or instruments in planes then, travel was restricted to daylight hours. Trains continued to move the mail at night.

The Post Office and its interest in delivering mail more quickly and efficiently were instrumental in the development of scheduled air service in the United States.

Soon the Post Office installed radio stations at small airfields for better communication. Finally, in 1921, new technology allowed flying by night and a nonstop journey from San Francisco to Long Island (in New York State) took place. The coast-to-coast trip was speedy compared to railroad standards: it took thirty-three hours and twenty-one minutes. Today, flying coast to coast takes about five hours.

CHAPTER 5

THE PONY EXPRESS

S kinny young men, galloping horses, Indian raids, wild-animal attacks, blizzards, and searing desert heat distinguished the most romantic mode of mail delivery: the Pony Express. It chewed up riders and mounts, lost money, and lasted just eighteen months. But the Pony Express helped link the eastern and western United States and created thrilling legends of courage and adventure.

California, which was admitted to the Union in 1848, provided the incentive for faster coast-to-coast mail service. Gold was discovered at Sutter's Mill in California the same year, spurring a rush of pioneers. As the state grew—from 1,000 residents in 1848 to 250,000 four years later—Californians began demanding better mail service. After all, it had taken six weeks for people in Los Angeles to hear from Washington,

This Frederic Remington painting shows the Pony
Express rider speeding away on a fresh mount.

D.C., that California had been made a state. The government sent mail south by ship from New York to the
east coast of Panama, inland across the isthmus, and
then by boat up to San Francisco. The trip took at
least twenty-two days.

The Central Overland California and Pike's Peak Express Company answered the demand for faster service by establishing the Pony Express. The new company hoped to snare government mail contracts. On April 3, 1860, booming cannons and cheering crowds launched riders at both ends of the 1,966-mile (3,164-km) route, in Sacramento, California, and St. Joseph, Missouri. The trip took ten days over plains and mountains and across rivers.

"Boston" Upson, the first rider from the East, was typical of the Pony Express men. He was twenty years old, 5 feet (152 cm) tall, and brave. With his mochila (a saddle cover with four mail pockets) draped over his horse, he charged across the high hump of the Sierra

Pony Express service promised delivery of mail from New York to San Francisco, a continent away, in a mere ten days.

Nevada. His horse collapsed in a snowbank, and he walked the last 3 miles (5 km), but even so, he completed his leg of the trip in eight hours—faster than a summer stagecoach could make it.

Along the route were twenty-five home stations where, in two minutes, the rider tossed the mochila to his replacement on a fresh horse. There were 165 swing stations where riders changed horses every 15 miles (24 km). Four hundred horses, two hundred station keepers and stablemen, and eighty tough riders were part of a system that moved thirty-five thousand pieces of mail over 650,000 miles (1,046,000 km) in eighteen months.

Buffalo stampedes, wolf attacks, Indian raids, and terrible weather were constant companions, but only one rider died, and none ever turned back.

In early 1861, it was not certain whether California would remain in the Union, or secede as the southern states were doing. The state's decision depended in part on policies that President Abraham Lincoln would set out in his inaugural address. Californians needed to hear the speech quickly. "Pony Bob" Haslam got the telegraphed address in St. Joseph, and with a pistol in each hand he set out on his horse across Indian territory. In a 2-mile (3-km) attack he caught an arrow in his arm, and another in his jaw knocked out five teeth. He pulled into a relay station and said, "Fetch me a clean rag to hold in my mouth—

The Pony Express rider salutes the workers who were constructing the telegraph poles that would shortly put the rider out of work.

I'm going through." Seven days and seventeen hours later, Lincoln's words reached Sacramento.

The speed was impressive, but the use of the telegraph was moving west. By October 1861, all the poles were in place and wires connected east and west. As we all know, the telegraph (like the telephone that came later), for all its speed—sending a message by telegraph was nearly instantaneous—would not eliminate the need for ordinary mail. But the Pony Express's main reason for being was its speed in delivering the written word, and in that it could not compete with the telegraph. And so, just eighteen months after its romantic birth, the Pony Express died.

CHAPTER 6

CIVIL WAR DAYS

The turmoil around the issue of slavery grew until war between the states was inevitable. The Civil War tore the young nation apart, but ironically it proved to be an opportunity for the mail system to improve.

The Post Office was chaotic and ineffective when President Abraham Lincoln appointed Montgomery Blair postmaster general in 1861. The appointment was an attempt to balance political power between the free and slave states. Blair was from Maryland, a border state that, like Kansas and Missouri, had influence because of its location.

Blair's first challenge was to hang on to post offices in the states that had seceded from the Union. But the Confederacy quickly included them in a system of its own. Meeting the mail demands of a coun-

The Union army generated massive amounts of mail
that taxed the ingenuity of the Post Office.

try at war with a disorganized system wasn't easy.
The Army was the biggest customer, and the volume
of mail it created caused changes .

Many post offices were in small towns, and when
an Army unit set up camp nearby, letters flooded in.
So did soldiers in search of stamps and mail from
home. To lessen the chaos, Blair let every regiment
appoint a postmaster who could distribute mail and
sell stamps and money orders. Later in the war, soldiers were granted the privilege of franking, or send-

ing letters free, a custom the U.S. government would follow in all later wars.

Money orders were a new thing, a way for soldiers to send their paychecks back home safely. Eventually they became available to the general public.

Postmaster Blair tightened basic regulations. Letters without prepaid postage could no longer be delivered. And with new indelible ink for cancellations, the old money-saving but dishonest trick of washing marks from stamps so they looked like they hadn't been used became impossible.

The amount of postage required depended on the weight of mail and how far it traveled. A single-sheet letter sent 40 miles (64 km) cost six or eight cents and one sent 400 miles (640 km) cost twenty-five cents. The cost rose two, three, or four times for extra sheets, which were folded over and addressed. (No one used envelopes.) In most parts of the country, sending and receiving letters meant a trip to the post office. Only in big cities did postmen deliver mail to private homes and businesses, which cost the recipient a few extra pennies.

In 1863, to make the Post Office more professional and efficient, Congress ordered a standard letter rate without regard to distance. It also began paying salaries to postmasters so they wouldn't have to rely on commissions on the mail they handled.

Despite the improvements, sometimes the mail didn't get through, as the story of the Reverend Samuel Ward of Neoga, Illinois, demonstrates. The minister wrote a letter to Professor W.D. Ward of Zanesville, Ohio, on November 11, 1860, the same day, he noted, that he cast his vote for "good Abe Lincoln." The letter was finally postmarked in 1910. It was just about as old as the Reverend Ward was when he first mailed it.

In big cities, boxes where mail could be collected began to show up on streets in the late 1850s. In 1863, free mail delivery started in forty-nine cities on July 1, coincidentally the same day the Battle of Gettysburg began. The sender still had to pay for postage, but recipients no longer paid an extra fee to mail carriers.

Street boxes for the collection of mail began to appear along city streets in the late 1850s.

CHAPTER 7

MARCHING TOWARD THE TURN OF THE CENTURY

T he nineteenth century was the golden era of the railroad. Those iron horses puffed their way across the continent, generating new settlements in their paths and connecting people and places as they advanced.

Up through the Civil War, the route agents on mail trains collected pouches at each rail stop, removed the local letters, and sent the rest along to be distributed through larger post offices. But gradually, the idea of sorting mail as it rolled along the tracks took shape.

The Railroad Post Office officially began in Illinois in August 1864. Route agents kept on handling local mail as they always had, but now they sent the rest to distribution centers on trains instead of those in cities. The speed of the rails and the ever widening

To speed along the delivery of mail
carried by rail, the Post Office established
special rail cars for the sorting of mail.

routes peaked in the twentieth century, and by 1930
more than 10,000 trains were involved in delivering
mail. But as airplane service increased, the Post
Office's dependence on the rails decreased.

In 1889, a Philadelphia retailer who believed in giv-
ing customers what they wanted, John Wanamaker,

became postmaster general. For the next four years he shook up the system to make it stronger. Some of his ideas were so far ahead of their time that they didn't take hold until much later.

Wanamaker's philosophy, as he put it, was "to keep the mail bag open to the latest possible minute, then get it to its destination in the shortest possible time, and then get each separate piece of mail to the person for whom it is meant in the quickest possible way."

The postcard made its debut during Wanamaker's tenure. So did letter chutes in hotels and collection boxes in clubs. Mail boxes sprouted on private homes, city streetcars became mail cars, and mail began to be sorted on transatlantic steamers. Wanamaker believed that postal patrons had a right to the best service possible, and he encouraged his employees to see that they got it.

One new way to speed delivery, using the pneumatic tube, was introduced in 1893, in Philadelphia. Cylinders holding mail were pushed by air pressure short distances from main post offices to smaller branches. The method became popular in many cities—more than half of New York City's mail was moved this way at one time. Use of pneumatic systems to move mail died out in the 1950s, when the method was replaced by modern technology that did the job better.

Postmaster John Wanamaker established pneumatic tube systems in large cities for the delivery of mail between the post offices and office buildings.

Toward the end of the century, the free delivery stopped being a privilege solely of city and town dwellers. In 1896, rural free delivery, or RFD, was born, bringing mail directly to the homes of farmers and other people living in the country.

Until then, people living in rural areas had to go into town to pick up their mail. For some the trip took several hours, or maybe even days. In those days before telephones, radios, and televisions, farmers and their families felt isolated, alone, and out of touch

Rural free delivery (RFD), established in 1896, brought those Americans living in the country closer to the rest of the world.

with the world much of the time. RFD helped to bring them into the mainstream.

RFD also had a tremendous, unforeseen impact on the highway system all over the United States. At first, free service to farmers was limited, because roads to their homes were hard to travel over. When farmers petitioned their local governments for help, new roads were built and old ones were improved. The resulting system of roads and highways not only improved mail delivery but made travel and shipment of goods easier for everyone. The new highways helped to make people feel a closer kinship with their fellow Americans.

CHAPTER 8

STAMPS AND POSTMARKS

For a long time after the U.S. mail system was up and running over the post roads, collecting the fees for postage was a problem. The sender paid for a letter to go from post office to post office. When home delivery started, instead of receiving a salary, the carrier collected an extra few cents from the person who received the letter. But often the person either didn't want the letter or couldn't afford the fee, and then the postman didn't get paid.

Making people pay in advance was a way for postmasters to stop losing money. By the 1840s, many of them were issuing their own stamps, called "postmaster provisionals." In 1847, Congress approved the first adhesive postage stamps for the whole country: a ten-cent stamp depicting George Washington and a

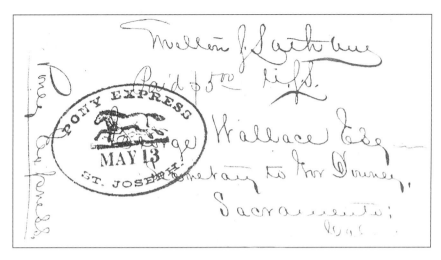

This postmark is a rare example of those
used on mail carried by the Pony Express.

five-cent depicting Benjamin Franklin. But prepaying
postage wasn't enforced until 1856.

Different services required different fees. There
were stamps for regular mail, special delivery, regis-
tered mail, insured mail, certified mail, and receipt
requested.

The custom of marking a letter to show the
postage had been paid — the postmark — started
before 1700. It was done by hand until 1772. After that,
a handstamp showed where the letter was mailed and
often told how it traveled, whether by Pony Express,
steamboat, or some other way.

Stamps are still used to pay for mail delivery, but

Examples of the first two United States postage stamps

many of them are also saved by collectors. Stamp collecting, or philately (the word comes from the Greek *philos* for "friend" and *ateleia* for "deliverance"), is a popular hobby. You can learn a great deal about geography and the way people live by collecting stamps.

Regular-issue stamps are the standard stickers that wear their value in a low-key way. The fun comes with commemorative stamps. They're issued specially to honor prominent people who are no longer alive, an event, an important anniversary, or a group of people. They're usually colorful and interesting to look at. Commemoratives have limited printings, and once they're gone, no more are printed.

Serious collectors are always searching for mis-

The Curtiss Jenny stamp is a very famous example of
the printing error on a postage stamp that was acci-
dentally released to the public. Today it is worth hundreds of thousands of times its original face value.

takes that make a stamp different and therefore valuable. Sometimes a batch will be printed with a miss-
pelled word, or the wrong color, or the incorrect
valuation. Sometimes there's a mark in the wrong position, or an error in the engraving. There have even
been cases of the design being printed upside down.

That happened to a limited run of a stamp honoring Charles Lindbergh, who in 1927 became the first
pilot to fly across the Atlantic. Years later, his Curtiss
Jenny airplane was reproduced on a two-color
stamp—upside down. Today that stamp is worth
$100,000 or more.

Commemorative stamps are special limited issues
that often become highly prized by collectors. This
sheet of stamps, "Legends of the West," is collectible
because of the wrong portrait of Bill Pickett
(second row, second from the left).

Hundreds of people flood the Postal Service with stamp ideas, but only about thirty new stamps are issued each year. A group called the Citizens' Stamp Advisory Committee meets every other month to look over new design suggestions. The postmaster general decides what will finally become a stamp based on the recommendations from the Advisory Committee.

The Post Office issued the first commemorative series—stamps honoring the four-hundredth anniversary of Columbus's voyage to America—in 1893. Since then, not only events, but all kinds of people have been honored: popular writers and artists and famous historians, explorers, black leaders, and women. Birds and flowers have also been commemorated. Among the most popular was the ten-cent moon-landing stamp issued in 1969. Perhaps it was so popular because the astronauts had carried with them the steel die for plates that were used to print the design.

In 1992, the Postal Service broke tradition by letting the public decide which of two possible versions of an Elvis Presley stamp would be issued, and millions of people made their wishes known. An image of the younger, slimmer Elvis won out over the rock and roll singer in his later days. More than one billion Elvis stamps were sold. The stamp will probably go down in history as the most popular of all time.

CHAPTER 9

THE POSTAL SERVICE TODAY

The Postal Service handles an enormous amount of mail every day—about 165 billion pieces. The load is a mix of personal letters, bills, business correspondence, newspapers, magazines, parcels, and third-class advertising pieces, sometimes called "junk mail." All this mail keeps postal employees working around the clock.

Until 1963, human beings had to read each piece of mail that came to the post office and decide where it was going. That was a slow process. Since then, ZIP codes, bar codes, and machines that read these codes do a lot of the work. They do it much faster, too.

Every address has a five-digit ZIP code, the numbers that show the district where you live or work. Instead of sorting mail by hand, postal workers just scan addresses for the ZIP codes on thousands of let-

This bar code sorting machine in Long Island, New York, represents the latest in technology for moving mail speedily across the nation.

ters each day. They then type the ZIP codes into a letter sorting machine (LSM) that can sort one letter per second.

Even faster are the machines that read bar codes. Bar codes are the tiny lines on the envelope that represent an address. The electric eye of an optical character reader (OCR) machine scans the address and then sprays a bar code on the envelope at the rate of about five hundred letters every minute.

Next, the bar code sorter (BCS) machine classifies

bar-coded mail. An operator feeds letters in, and the machine reads and sorts them by town or by street. The mail goes into trays that are loaded onto trucks or planes.

Automation—the use of machines to do work that would otherwise be done by people — also keeps costs down so everyone can afford to use the Postal Service. Sorting one thousand pieces of mail would cost forty-two dollars if it were done by hand. Machines have slashed that cost to only three dollars.

The Postal Service needs to be as efficient as possible so all that mail will be delivered in a reasonable amount of time. The American people demand good service. The Postal Service decided that adding four numbers to each ZIP code would more accurately identify addresses and further speed the sorting of mail. Now everyone has the new nine-digit code, known as the ZIP+4 number.

The busiest times for postal workers are when the rest of us are asleep. More than 200,000 workers begin work at midnight in central collection post offices. They have just five hours to go through all the mail and sort it by ZIP code for delivery.

By sunrise, the day's mail is at local post offices. There, letter carriers organize their own routes and deliver to their customers during the day. There are approximately 232,000 city carriers and 43,000 rural carriers who cover routes that stretch 2.6 million

Truck drivers work through the night (and bad weather!) to move mail and packages from city to city.

miles (4.2 million km). These workers deliver an average of 550 pieces of mail each day.

There are many ways to send your mail. When you put a twenty-nine-cent stamp on a letter weighing up to 1 ounce (28 g), you're sending it first class, and it will usually be delivered in one to three days. Heavier first-class letters will cost you more (the heavier the letter, the greater the cost). Second-class, third-class, and fourth-class mail usually cost less and take a little longer.

A new category of service, Express Mail, is more

expensive, but mail sent in this fashion is guaranteed to be delivered in a certain amount of time, usually overnight. Another new category for faster delivery is Priority Mail, which is much less expensive than Express Mail but is also slower. Although the Postal Service tries to deliver Priority Mail within two days, it doesn't guarantee that delivery won't take longer. When you must get something to someone in a hurry, Priority Mail and Express Mail are good ways to go.

Benjamin Franklin would probably be amazed if he could stroll through a city mail distribution center today. It's not likely that the Father of the U.S. Postal Service could ever have imagined the amount of mail handled every day, the numbers of people it takes to move it, or the kinds of machinery that help do the job.

Ben Franklin might also be surprised that his old job is no longer a presidential cabinet position. On July 1, 1971, Congress passed the Postal Reorganization Act creating the U.S. Postal Service (the original agency was called the U.S. Post Office), an independent government agency operated by a nine-member Board of Governors. They, not the president, appoint the postmaster general.

The Postal Service is the biggest employer in the land. It has 40,000 post offices, stations, and branches, 750,000 workers, and about 176,000 vehicles.

CHAPTER 10

BITS AND PIECES

An organization with as long a history as the Postal Service's has lots of funny, sad, interesting, and odd stories to tell. The mail has created plenty of jokes, like this one about a woman who was shocked to find her letter carrier throwing his mailbag at her dog. She quickly opened a window and yelled out: "Hey, leave my dog alone. He won't bite. In fact, he doesn't even bark," she yelled. "I know he can't bark, lady," said the carrier. "He's got my leg in his mouth!"

Sometimes, delivering the mail is a dangerous and complicated job. A carrier in Miami, Florida, who traveled his route on a bike fell off one day—and into an ants' nest. The ants swarmed into his pants and up his shirt. In desperation, the carrier pulled his clothes off. The mail got through, but the carrier was fined $50 for indecent exposure.

There are many stories about lost mail. One of them was told at the end of Chapter 6. Here's another: A man in a Minneapolis, Minnesota, company mailed a letter to a man in Pingree, North Dakota, in 1907. It was finally delivered twenty years later, with an added note: "Recovered from a crevice in back of a mail chute in the Chamber of Commerce building, January 27, 1927." In the meantime both men had moved to California, where they met.

There are crazy stories, too. Parcel post began in 1913. In Idaho, May Pierstorf's parents thought it would be cheaper to mail their four-year-old daughter to her grandmother than buy a train ticket for her. She fit the weight requirements—she was 2 pounds (0.9 kg) under the 50-pound (22.7-kg) limit. They classified her as a baby chick, which you could legally send by parcel post. They glued fifty-three cents' worth of stamps to a tag on May's coat and she rode in the mail-baggage car to Lewiston, Idaho. A clerk delivered her to her grandmother.

One animal who rode legally in mail cars all the time was Owney, the mascot of the railway mail service. He was an Irish terrier who wandered into the Albany, New York, post office in the fall of 1888 and snuggled down on a pile of old mailbags. Pretty soon he was a regular passenger on the wagons moving the mail from the post office to the railway depot.

Everyone loved Owney. And he loved perching on

The world-traveling mail dog, Owney

the mail, wherever it went. One time, he rode with it from Albany to New York City. He was hooked, and soon he was traveling all over the country. Postal workers always took care of him.

Owney eventually traveled around the world. He boarded a ship in Tacoma, Washington, with a little suitcase that held his soft blanket, a brush, and a comb. He went to Japan, China, Singapore, Suez, Algiers, and the Azores before he steamed into New York. The entire trip lasted 132 days. Today you can see the stuffed Owney at the Smithsonian Institution in Washington, D.C.

Maybe Owney sensed how important letters are to people. They've always been an important link to families, especially during wartime. Here's one from a little girl to her father in the Persian Gulf during

Desert Storm. "Dear Dad. When you left I thought I was going to lose you so don't get hurt. Dad, when you get back I won't be sucking my thumb anymore just for you."

Another Desert Storm soldier wrote this bad news to his mother from the Persian Gulf: "I finally found out why I haven't heard from Tara. I called her house last night and the first time she hung up on me. The second time I called, a guy answered the phone and said: 'She's got a new boyfriend' and hung up."

Whatever the news, and whatever the circumstances, a letter is special. "What a pleasing thing it is to receive letters from our friends," wrote Lorenzo Vanderhoef, a Civil War soldier. "During this war while so many of our dearest friends are away on the tented field, what hours and weeks of dreadful anxiety we would be obliged to endure were it not that we have a medium for communication with them. . . ."

The telephone has made communication so easy that people don't write letters as much as they used to. That's too bad. There's nothing as special as a letter. It's a gift filled with news and opinions and feelings, and it shows that someone cares.

Write a letter today. Write to a friend or a cousin or your grandmother or to your newspaper. And when you mail it, think of how it will be carried along on the rich history of the United States Postal Service.

FOR FURTHER READING

Brandt, Betty. *Special Delivery.* Minneapolis: Carol-
   rhoda Books, 1987.
Gibbons, Gail. *The Post Office Book*: Mail and How It
   Moves. New York: Harper & Row, 1986.
Mackay, James A. *The Guiness Book of Stamps: Facts &
   Feats.* New York: Canopy Books, 1992.

INDEX

ABOUT THE
AUTHOR

Nancy O'Keefe Bolick is the corporate communications manager for a small environmental company and is a freelance writer. She has taught English in senior and junior high school, and currently she is a part-time instructor of commercial writing for business people. Her previously published books for young adults were on the inventions and villages of the Shakers.

She and her husband live in Massachusetts and have two children, one a teenager and one a young adult.